MAP OF BURKINA FASO

Burkina Faso

———	International boundary
—·—·—	Province boundary
★	National capital
⊚	Province capital
———	Railroad
———	Road

0   25   50   75   100 Kilometers
0   25   50   75   100 Miles
Lambert Conformal Conic Projection, SP 8N/32N

MALI

NIGER

Niger

Gao

Gossi

Ménaka

Ansongo

Douentza

Ayorou

Tillabéri

15

Téra

Niamey

OUDALAN

Gorom Gorom

Aribinda

SOUM

Djibo

Dori

SÉNO

YATENGA

Ouahigouya

Séguénéga

BAM

Kongoussi

SANMATENGA

Tougan

SOUROU

Yako

PASSORE

Kaya

GNAGNA

Bogandé

Nouna

KOSSI

Dédougou

NAMENTENGA

Boulsa

Kantchari

Tapoa

Koutiala

Koury

OUBRITENGA

Ziniaré

KADIOGO

BOULKIEMDE

Réo

Koudougou

Ouagadougou

GANZOURGOU

Zorgo

Kpupèla

KOURITENGA

Fada-N'Gourma

Diapaga

MOUHOUN

SANGUIÉ

Boromo

Kombissiri

BAZÉGA

Toéssé

Manga

GOURMA

TAPOA

12

Tenkodogo

BOULGOU

KÉNÉDOUGOU

Houndé

SISSILI

ZOUNDWÉOGO

Pama

Bobo-Dioulasso

HOUET

Léo

NAOURI

Pô

Orodara

Diébougou

Navrongo

Bawku

Dapaong

Banfora

BOUGOURIBA

Tumu

Bolgatanga

Tanguiéta

Natitingou

KOMOÉ

Gaoua

PONI

Wa

Wulugu

Mango

BÉNIN

Varalé

Kanté

TOGO

Ferkessédougou

Bouna

Tamale

Yendi

Kara

Djougou

GHANA

Bassar

Bole

Tchamba

CÔTE

Koutouba

Sokodé

Dabakala

Salaga

Sotouboua

Blitta

D'IVOIRE

9

Katiola

Bamboi

Kintampo

Dumbai

Savalou

Bouaké

Bondoukou

Kwadjokrom

Kéte Krachi

Atakpamé

Berekum

Lake Volta

Lac de Kossou

Base 802455 (A01009) 3-96

TABLE OF CONTENTS

CORE EXPECTATIONS
FOR PEACE CORPS VOLUNTEERS

In working toward fulfilling the Peace Corps Mission of promoting world peace and friendship, as a trainee and Volunteer, you are expected to:

1. Prepare your personal and professional life to make a commitment to serve abroad for a full term of 27 months

2. Commit to improving the quality of life of the people with whom you live and work; and, in doing so, share your skills, adapt them, and learn new skills as needed

3. Serve where the Peace Corps asks you to go, under conditions of hardship, if necessary, and with the flexibility needed for effective service

4. Recognize that your successful and sustainable development work is based on the local trust and confidence you build by living in, and respectfully integrating yourself into, your host community and culture

5. Recognize that you are responsible 24 hours a day, 7 days a week for your personal conduct and professional performance

6. Engage with host country partners in a spirit of cooperation, mutual learning, and respect

7. Work within the rules and regulations of the Peace Corps and the local and national laws of the country where you serve

8. Exercise judgment and personal responsibility to protect your health, safety, and well-being and that of others

9. Recognize that you will be perceived, in your host country and community, as a representative of the people, cultures, values, and traditions of the United States of America

10. Represent responsively the people, cultures, values, and traditions of your host country and community to people in the United States both during and following your service

PEACE CORPS/BURKINA FASO
HISTORY AND PROGRAMS

History of the Peace Corps in Burkina Faso

The Peace Corps entered Burkina Faso, then called Upper Volta, in 1966. Programs included small enterprise development, education, agriculture, and environment. In 1987, Peace Corps ceased operations in Burkina Faso due to the government's development policies no longer aligning with Peace Corps goals. After a change in government administration and policies, the Peace Corps was invited back to Burkina Faso in 1995 to begin a health program. Programs in education and small enterprise development were established in 1996 and 2003, respectively. Currently, nearly 150 Volunteers work throughout the country. Approximately 2,000 Peace Corps Volunteers have served in Burkina Faso to date.

History and Future of Peace Corps Programming in Burkina Faso

Peace Corps/Burkina Faso works within three program areas: health, education, and community economic development. These projects were recently revised, taking into account the country's needs and the comparative advantage of using Volunteers. Health Volunteers' primary responsibilities are to work in close collaboration with local health clinic staff to raise awareness on topics such as maternal and child health, malaria, hygiene, nutrition, family planning, and HIV/AIDS for people living in their communities. Education Volunteers use participatory student-centered approaches to teach math, science, information, and communication technologies, and life skills at primary and junior-high school levels. After-school programs such as clubs, tutoring, and camps that generate awareness on life-skills and gender equality are also facilitated by education Volunteers. Community economic development Volunteers help farmers increase their business skills and knowledge in an effort to develop profitable and sustainable income-generating activities such as gardens, woodlots, and animal husbandry and transforming post harvest crops into market products.

COUNTRY OVERVIEW:
BURKINA FASO AT A GLANCE

History

Most of the area known today as Burkina Faso was once dominated by the Mossi people, who established their empire around 1500. In 1897, France imposed its rule over the people of Burkina Faso, but it was not until 1947 that the French colony of Haute Volta (Upper Volta) was created. Full independence from the French came on August 5, 1960, with Maurice Yaméogo as the nation's first president.

Four of the six presidents after Yaméogo came into power through military coups. Thomas Sankara, who, after a coup, led the country from August 1983 until his death on October 15, 1987, was arguably the most influential of Burkina Faso's presidents. Sankara's charismatic leadership style, which emphasized self-sufficiency and a lean and efficient government that transferred wealth from urban centers to rural areas, was popular with citizens, and created a sense of hope in the country. In 1984, the country's name was changed from Upper Volta to Burkina Faso: "Country of the Upright/Honorable People."

The current president, Blaise Compaore, has been in power since Sankara's death. Compaore led four years of military rule, then was the only candidate in the presidential election; he was sworn-in as president of the fourth republic on December 24, 1991. Compaore has won the last two presidential elections, held in 1998 and 2005, by wide margins.

Government

Burkina Faso is an independent republic with a unicameral National Assembly of 112 members (called deputies) who serve five-year terms. Political and constitutional reforms have moved Burkina Faso incrementally toward democratization. In 1991, a new constitution was passed through a referendum, laying the foundation of the fourth republic.

Economy

Burkina Faso has few natural resources, and 90 percent of the population engages in subsistence agriculture producing peanuts, sesame, cotton, sorghum, millet, corn, and rice, and raising livestock. Agricultural production is limited and risky because of poor soil and cyclical droughts. A significant portion of the labor force migrates annually to neighboring coastal countries in search of unskilled employment. The primary exports, cotton and livestock, are subject to major price and yield fluctuations. Burkina Faso is classified as one of the poorest countries in the world. The country ranked 181 out of 187 in the 2011 United Nations Human Development Index.

People and Culture

The population of Burkina Faso is approximately 13.9 million, with an annual growth rate of about 2.8 percent. Sharing borders with six countries, Burkina Faso is composed of a rich mix of people representing over 60 language or ethnic groups.

Islam is practiced by about 52 percent of the population; Christianity (Roman Catholicism and Protestantism) by about 18 percent; and indigenous beliefs, which play a major role in the lives of many Burkinabé regardless of their religious orientation, are held by approximately 30 percent. The Burkinabé are known for their tolerance and acceptance of ethnic and religious diversity. While Islam is practiced by a significant portion of the population, religious fundamentalism is rare.

The Pan-African Film and Television Festival of Ouagadougou and the International Arts and Crafts Show are two major events that highlight Burkina Faso as a country devoted to cultivating the arts. Artists and art connoisseurs from all over the world come to Burkina Faso for these events.

The people of Burkina Faso are the country's greatest resource. Despite their poverty, they remain dignified, extremely hardworking, and very welcoming to foreigners. Peace Corps Volunteers could not find a more hospitable group of people to work with than the Burkinabé.

Environment

Burkina Faso sits on the edge of the Sahel with an area of 105,869 square miles. It is bordered on the north by Mali and Niger and on the south by Côte d'Ivoire, Ghana, Togo, and Benin. While the north is mainly desert, the southern and central regions are forested. There are two distinct seasons in Burkina Faso: the rainy season from June to October and the dry season from November to May. The combination of population pressures and prolonged dry cycles has contributed to widespread environmental degradation, as indicated by declining vegetation cover, soil fertility, and land productivity.

RESOURCES FOR FURTHER INFORMATION

Following is a list of websites for additional information about the Peace Corps, Burkina Faso, and to connect you to returned Volunteers and other invitees. Please keep in mind that although we try to make sure all these links are active and current, we cannot guarantee it. If you do not have access to the Internet, visit your local library. Libraries offer free Internet usage and often let you print information to take home.

A note of caution: As you surf the Internet, be aware that you may find bulletin boards and chat rooms in which people are free to express opinions about the Peace Corps based on their own experience, including comments by those who were unhappy with their choice to serve in the Peace Corps. These opinions are not those of the Peace Corps or the U.S. government, and we hope you will keep in mind that no two people experience their service in the same way.

General Information About Burkina Faso

www.countrywatch.com

On this site, you can learn anything from what time it is in the capital of Burkina Faso to how to convert from the dollar to the Burkina Faso currency. Just click on Burkina Faso and go from there.

www.lonelyplanet.com/destinations

Visit this site for general travel advice about almost any country in the world.

www.state.gov

The State Department's website issues background notes periodically about countries around the world. Find Burkina Faso and learn more about its social and political history. You can also go to the site's international travel section to check on conditions that may affect your safety.

www.psr.keele.ac.uk/official.htm

This includes links to all the official sites for governments worldwide.

www.geography.about.com/library/maps/blindex.htm

This online world atlas includes maps and geographical information, and each country page contains links to other sites, such as the Library of Congress, that contain comprehensive historical, social, and political background.

www.cyberschoolbus.un.org/infonation/info.asp

This United Nations site allows you to search for statistical information for member states of the U.N.

www.worldinformation.com

This site provides an additional source of current and historical information about countries around the world.

Connect With Returned Volunteers and Other Invitees

www.rpcv.org

This is the site of the National Peace Corps Association, made up of returned Volunteers. On this site you can find links to all the Web pages of the "Friends of" groups for most countries of service, comprised of former Volunteers who served in those countries. There are also regional groups that frequently get together for social events and local volunteer activities. Or go straight to the Friends of Burkina Faso site: **http://fbf.tamu.edu/**

www.PeaceCorpsWorldwide.org

This site is hosted by a group of returned Volunteer writers. It is a monthly online publication of essays and Volunteer accounts of their Peace Corps service.

Online Articles/Current News Sites About Burkina Faso

www.primature.gov.bf

This is the government of Burkina Faso website (in French).

www.fespaco.bf

This is the site of the Pan-African Film and Television Festival of Ouagadougou (in French or English), which takes place in Burkina Faso every two years.

www.sas.upenn.edu/African_Studies/Country_Specific/Burkina.html

This Burkina Faso page from the University of Pennsylvania's African Studies Center also links to other sites of interest.

http://www-sul.stanford.edu/depts/ssrg/africa/burkina/burkinanews.html

This Stanford University-based site on the region also links to a variety of other sites.

www.allafrica.com

The All Africa Global Media site is a news and information service.

www.uiowa.edu/~africart

This site for the Art and Life in Africa Project of the University of Iowa was set up by returned Burkina Faso Volunteer Chris Roy, a professor of art history and specialist on Voltaic masks.

International Development Sites About Burkina Faso

www.unaids.org

Joint United Nations Programme on HIV/AIDS

www.unicef.org

UNICEF

www.who.int/en

World Health Organization

www.pnud.bf

United Nations Development Programme (in French)

Recommended Books

- Chilson, Peter. *Riding the Demon: On the Road in West Africa.* Athens: University of Georgia Press, 1999.

- Else, David, et al. *West Africa.* Oakland, Calif.: Lonely Planet, 1999.

- Englebert, Pierre. *Burkina Faso: Unsteady Statehood in West Africa.* Boulder, Colo.: Westview Press, 1995.

- Guirma, Frederic. *Tales of Mogho: African Stories from Upper Volta.* New York: Macmillan, 1971.

- Rupley, Lawrence, and Daniel Miles McFarland. *Historical Dictionary of Burkina Faso* (2nd ed.). Lanham, Md.: Scarecrow Press, 1998.

- Knight, James, and Katrina Manson. *Burkina Faso: The Bradt Travel Guide.* Bradt Travel Guides, 2006.

Books About the History of the Peace Corps

- Hoffman, Elizabeth Cobbs. *All You Need is Love: The Peace Corps and the Spirit of the 1960s.* Cambridge, Mass.: Harvard University Press, 2000.

- Rice, Gerald T. *The Bold Experiment: JFK's Peace Corps.* Notre Dame, Ind.: University of Notre Dame Press, 1985.

- Stossel, Scott. *Sarge: The Life and Times of Sargent Shriver*. Washington, D.C.: Smithsonian Institution Press, 2004.

- Meisler, Stanley. *When the World Calls: The Inside Story of the Peace Corps and its First 50 Years*. Boston, Mass.: Beacon Press, 2011.

Books on the Volunteer Experience

- Dirlam, Sharon. *Beyond Siberia: Two Years in a Forgotten Place*. Santa Barbara, Calif.: McSeas Books, 2004.

- Casebolt, Marjorie DeMoss. *Margarita: A Guatemalan Peace Corps Experience*. Gig Harbor, Wash.: Red Apple Publishing, 2000.

- Erdman, Sarah. Nine Hills to Nambonkaha: Two Years in the Heart of an African Village. New York, N.Y.: Picador, 2003.

- Hessler, Peter. *River Town: Two Years on the Yangtze*. New York, N.Y.: Perennial, 2001.

- Kennedy, Geraldine ed. *From the Center of the Earth: Stories out of the Peace Corps*. Santa Monica, Calif.: Clover Park Press, 1991.

- Thompsen, Moritz. *Living Poor: A Peace Corps Chronicle*. Seattle, Wash.: University of Washington Press, 1997 (reprint).

LIVING CONDITIONS AND VOLUNTEER LIFESTYLE

Communications

Despite Burkina Faso's relatively good communications systems, you should be prepared for a significant reduction in the frequency and reliability of your communications with friends and family, lengthy delays between letters, the lack of nearby telephones, and uncertain access to email.

Mail

The postal system in Burkina Faso is reliable by African standards. Few Volunteers report problems receiving letters sent from the United State by airmail, however packages have arrived damaged or gone missing. Airmail letters and packages typically take three to four weeks to arrive, but can take longer if there are mail strikes or other disruptions. Surface mail is not currently available from the United States to Burkina Faso. Internal mail service is reliable for the most part, with mail delivered within a few days to two weeks.

Essential documents are best sent via a courier service, such as DHL. Please note, however, that items sent via courier service or packages sent via the post incur customs fees, which need to be paid on the Burkina side before receiving the package. These fees run anywhere from $1 for a small package through the post to $100 for a large package through DHL. The Peace Corps will usually pay these fees up front and deduct them from your living allowance. You can receive mail at the Peace Corps office or at your site through a local post box. During pre-service training, you should have mail sent in care of the Peace Corps office to the following address:

> "Your Name," PCT
> S/c Corps de la Paix
> 01 B.P. 6031 Ouagadougou 01, Burkina Faso

Telephones

Telephone service in Burkina Faso is relatively reliable. A number of Volunteers have access to phone service at their sites through land-line phones at telecenters. **Cell phone** service is expanding rapidly and most Volunteer sites are now

Computer, Internet, and Email Access

Computer access is available at private Internet cafes in many towns and cities and, for work-related purposes, at the Peace Corps office. Wireless coverage, when available, can be slow. Unlocked smart phones can provide Internet access almost anywhere. In smaller villages, there may not be electricity, but there are almost always places to charge electronic equipment for a small fee.

Housing and Site Location

Your community or the government ministry to which you are assigned will provide you with safe and adequate housing in accordance with the Peace Corps' site selection criteria. The majority of health and community economic development Volunteers live in small rural villages, while education Volunteers tend to live in larger villages and towns. Volunteer housing is typically a small house made of mud or cement bricks with a thatch or tin roof. Many Volunteers do not have running water or electricity; they draw their water from a well and obtain light through kerosene lanterns. Nearly all Volunteers are within a couple hours from a neighboring Volunteer and able to reach the Peace Corps office in Ouagadougou by public transport within a day.

Living Allowance and Money Management

Peace Corps/Burkina Faso covers the cost of Volunteers' basic living and professional expenses, including a vacation allowance equivalent to $24 a month. The Peace Corps opens a checking account for each Volunteer that can be accessed at several post offices around the country.

The current living allowance is approximately $240 per month. The Peace Corps also gives Volunteers a quarterly allowance for work-related travel of approximately $60. All of these allowances are paid in the local currency, the CFA franc.

The amount of the living allowance is based on an annual survey of Volunteers' financial needs. Most Volunteers report they have no trouble living comfortably on this allowance.

If the Peace Corps asks you to travel, you will be given additional money for transportation and meals. The amount is established by the director of management and operations based on the cost of transportation and lodging.

Food and Diet

Your drinking water is likely to be of poor quality and thus will require boiling and filtering (the Peace Corps will provide you with filters). The variety of fruits and vegetables is somewhat limited, with only one fruit or vegetable often available during any given season. Burkina Faso produces some of the best mangoes and papayas in the world, but they are seasonal. Garlic, onions, tomatoes, and a local variety of eggplant are available year-round in many locations. Other fruits and vegetables grown in the country, depending on the season and location, include oranges, grapefruits, bananas, carrots, cabbages, potatoes, beets, lettuce, and cucumbers. Burkinabé meals are simple. A typical dish consists of a staple food such as rice, millet, yams, sorghum, or maize served with a sauce made from okra, various greens (e.g., spinach), tomatoes, and/or peanuts. Sauces may contain fish or meat. French bread is available in larger towns and villages.

Transportation

Paved roads connect the largest towns and cities in Burkina Faso, and fairly well-maintained buses service these routes on a regular schedule. Smaller towns and villages are served by "bush taxis"—typically overcrowded and poorly maintained minibuses that do not run on a fixed schedule. Most Volunteers do not live near paved roads, preventing daily access to motorized transportation out of their villages. All Volunteers are issued basic mountain bikes for work purposes and must wear a bicycle helmet when cycling. **(Volunteers should purchase their helmets in the States and bring the receipt for reimbursement after arrival in-country.)** For safety reasons, Peace Corps/ Burkina Faso prohibits Volunteers from driving or riding on any two- or three-wheeled motorized vehicles (such as a motorcycle) except in a life-threatening emergency. Some Volunteers receive special authorization to ride as a passenger on a motorbike when necessary for work purposes. Please note that Volunteers are not allowed to own or drive any type of motorized vehicle in Burkina Faso.

Geography and Climate

Burkina Faso is slightly larger than Colorado. Its topography has little variation, consisting mainly of grassland with sparse forests. Many of the ecosystems found in West Africa are represented in Burkina Faso, from the forest zone in the south to savannah in the midlands to the Sahara Desert in the north. Burkina Faso is generally greener in the south because of its higher annual precipitation.

There is a rainy season from June to October, when most staple crops are grown, and a long dry season from November through May. The harmattan winds blow off the Sahara from November through March, a period characterized by dry, dusty conditions. Temperatures range from a cool and dry 50 degrees Fahrenheit (10 C) in November to a humid 104 degrees Fahrenheit (40 C) before the rains begin in June.

Social Activities

Social activities will vary according to where you are located. They might include relaxing and talking with friends and neighbors, going to the market, or taking part in local festivals. The cultural diversity of Burkina Faso means that there is always something of interest taking place nearby that you can learn from, be it drumming and dancing or planting peanuts. Many Volunteers meet periodically in regional market towns to share ideas and experiences. However, in keeping with its goal of cross-cultural exchange, the Peace Corps expects Volunteers to establish social networks with Burkinabé friends and colleagues at their sites rather than seek out other Volunteers for social activities. Such networks enhance Volunteers' ability to be effective in their work.

Professionalism, Dress, and Behavior

One of the biggest challenges faced by Volunteers in Burkina Faso is defining their role as professionals in the Burkinabé context. The tendency of Burkinabé counterparts to blur (from a Western perspective) the distinction between professional and personal time and space adds a layer of complexity to the challenge of establishing oneself as a professional. Cultivating work relationships is not something that happens only during work hours: Behavior and activities outside the work setting will have an impact on your professional relationships.

The Burkinabé, like many other Africans, put a great deal of emphasis upon dressing well in public, whether at work, in the market, or at a night spot. It is almost unheard of, for example, for a Burkinabé man or woman to wear shorts in public unless he or she is taking part in some kind of sporting event. Nor would a professional man or woman ever be seen wearing dirty, disheveled, wrinkled, or torn clothing.

Volunteers need to be aware of other unwritten rules of the culture, such as the fact that Burkinabé women never go to a bar on their own. Exposed body piercings on men and women or long hair on men may elicit stares and, possibly, rude questions or comments, so they are not advisable. Serving in the Peace Corps often requires sacrificing personal preferences regarding dress and behavior. There will be ample discussion of this subject during cross-cultural sessions in pre-service training.

Personal Safety

More detailed information about the Peace Corps' approach to safety is contained in the "Health Care and Safety" chapter, but it is an important issue and cannot be overemphasized. As stated in the Volunteer Handbook, becoming a Peace Corps Volunteer entails certain safety risks. Living and traveling in an unfamiliar environment (oftentimes alone), having a limited understanding of local language and culture, and being perceived as well-off are some of the factors that can put a Volunteer at risk. Many Volunteers experience varying degrees of unwanted attention and harassment. Petty thefts and burglaries are not uncommon, and incidents of physical and sexual assault do occur, although most Burkina Faso Volunteers complete their two years of service without incident. The Peace Corps has established procedures and policies designed to help you reduce your risks and enhance your safety and security. These procedures and policies, in addition to safety training, will be provided once you arrive in Burkina Faso. Using these tools, you are expected to take responsibility for your safety and well-being.

Each staff member at the Peace Corps is committed to providing Volunteers with the support they need to successfully meet the challenges they will face to have a safe, healthy, and productive service. We encourage Volunteers and families to look at our safety and security information on the Peace Corps website at **www.peacecorps.gov/safety**.

Information on these pages gives messages on Volunteer health and Volunteer safety. There is a section titled "Safety and Security – Our Partnership." Among topics addressed are the risks of serving as a Volunteer, posts' safety support systems, and emergency planning and communications.

Rewards and Frustrations

Although the potential for job satisfaction in Burkina Faso is quite high, like all Volunteers, you will encounter frustrations. Collaborating agencies may not always provide the support that has been promised; the pace of work and life is slow compared to life in America. For these reasons, the Peace Corps experience of adapting to a new culture and environment is often described as a series of emotional peaks and valleys. You will be given a high degree of responsibility and independence in your work—perhaps more than in any other job you have had or will have. You will often find yourself in situations that require an ability to motivate yourself and your co-workers with little guidance from supervisors. You might work for months without seeing any visible impact from, or without receiving feedback on, your work. You must possess the self-confidence, patience, and vision to continue working toward long-term goals without seeing immediate results. To overcome these difficulties, you will need maturity, flexibility, open-mindedness and resourcefulness. The Peace Corps staff, your Burkinabé co-workers, and fellow Volunteers will support you during times of challenge, as well as in moments of success. Judging by the experience of former Volunteers, the peaks are well worth the difficult times, and most Volunteers leave Burkina Faso feeling they have gained much more than they sacrificed during their service. If you are able to make the commitment to integrate into your community and work hard, you will be a successful Volunteer.

PEACE CORPS TRAINING

Pre-Service Training

Training is an essential part of Peace Corps service. The goal of the training program is to give you the skills and information you need to live and work effectively in Burkina Faso. In doing that, we build upon the experiences and expertise you bring to the Peace Corps. We anticipate that you will approach training with an open mind, a desire to learn, and a willingness to become involved. Trainees officially become Volunteers only after successful completion of training.

You will receive training and orientation in components of language, cross-culture, development issues, health, safety and security and technical skills pertinent to your specific assignment. Training combines structured classroom study, independent study, and hands-on experiences. The skills you learn will serve as the foundation upon which you build your experience as a Peace Corps Volunteer.

During the first couple days of training, you will stay at a hotel in the capital city of Ouagadougou (pronounced waga-dugu). After this orientation period, you will travel to Leo, where our training center is located, about 250 km south of Ouagadougou. Trainees will be assigned to a host family with whom they will live for the duration of pre-service training. The host family experience, which Volunteers in Burkina Faso consider one of the most valuable and critical elements of training, allows you to gain hands-on experience in some of the new skills you are expected to acquire.

Depending on your sector, your initial period of training will be either nine or eleven weeks. Those with the shorter period of pre-service training will attend a longer in-service training after three months of service.

Technical Training

Technical training will prepare you to work in Burkina Faso by building on the skills you already have and helping you develop new skills in a manner appropriate to the needs of the country. The Peace Corps staff, Burkina Faso experts, and current Volunteers will conduct the training program. Training places great emphasis on learning how to transfer the skills you have to the community in which you will serve as a Volunteer.

Technical training will include sessions on the general economic and political environment in Burkina Faso and strategies for working within such a framework. You will review your technical sector's goals and will meet with the Burkina Faso agencies and organizations that invited the Peace Corps to assist them. You will be supported and evaluated throughout the training to build the confidence and skills you need to undertake your project activities and be a productive member of your community.

Language Training

As a Peace Corps Volunteer, you will find that language skills are key to personal and professional satisfaction during your service. These skills are critical to your job performance, they help you integrate into your community, and they can ease your personal adaptation to the new surroundings. Therefore, language training is at the heart of the training program. You must successfully meet minimum language requirements to complete training and become a Volunteer. Burkina Faso language instructors teach formal language classes five days a week in small groups of four to five people.

Your language training will incorporate a community-based approach. In addition to classroom time, you will be given assignments to work on outside of the classroom and with your host family. The goal is to get you to a point of basic social communication skills so you can practice and develop language skills further once you are at your site. Prior to being sworn in as a Volunteer, you will work on strategies to continue language studies during your service.

Cross-Cultural Training

As part of your pre-service training, you will live with a Burkina Faso host family. This experience is designed to ease your transition to life at your site. Families go through an orientation conducted by Peace Corps staff to explain the purpose of pre-service training and to assist them in helping you adapt to living in Burkina Faso. Many Volunteers form strong and lasting friendships with their host families.

Cross-cultural and community development training will help you improve your communication skills and understand your role as a facilitator of development. You will be exposed to topics such as community mobilization, conflict resolution, gender and development, nonformal and adult education strategies, and political structures.

Health Training

During pre-service training, you will be given basic medical training and information. You will be expected to practice preventive health care and to take responsibility for your own health by adhering to all medical policies. Trainees are required to attend all medical sessions. The topics include preventive health measures and minor and major medical issues that you might encounter while in Burkina Faso. Nutrition, mental health, setting up a safe living compound, and how to avoid HIV/AIDS and other sexually transmitted diseases (STDs) are also covered.

Safety Training

During the safety training sessions, you will learn how to adopt a lifestyle that reduces your risks at home, at work, and during your travels. You will also learn appropriate, effective strategies for coping with unwanted attention and about your individual responsibility for promoting safety throughout your service.

Additional Trainings During Volunteer Service

In its commitment to institutionalize quality training, the Peace Corps has implemented a training system that provides Volunteers with continual opportunities to examine their commitment to Peace Corps service while increasing their technical and cross-cultural skills. During service, there are usually three training events. The titles and objectives for those trainings are as follows:

- In-service training: Provides an opportunity for Volunteers to upgrade their technical, language, and project development skills while sharing their experiences and reaffirming their commitment after having served for three to six months.

- Midterm conference (done in conjunction with technical sector in-service): Assists Volunteers in reviewing their first year, reassessing their personal and project objectives, and planning for their second year of service.

- Close-of-service conference: Prepares Volunteers for the future after Peace Corps service and reviews their respective projects and personal experiences.

The number, length, and design of these trainings are adapted to country-specific needs and conditions. The key to the training system is that training events are integrated and interrelated, from the pre-departure orientation through the end of your service, and are planned, implemented, and evaluated cooperatively by the training staff, Peace Corps staff, and Volunteers.

YOUR HEALTH CARE AND
SAFETY IN BURKINA FASO

The Peace Corps' highest priority is maintaining the good health and safety of every Volunteer. Peace Corps medical programs emphasize the preventive, rather than the curative, approach to disease. The Peace Corps in Burkina Faso maintains a clinic with a full-time medical officer, who takes care of Volunteers' primary health care needs. Additional medical services, such as testing and basic treatment, are also available in Burkina Faso at local hospitals. If you become seriously ill, you will be transported either to an American-standard medical facility in the region or to the United States.

Health Issues in Burkina Faso

Major health problems among Peace Corps Volunteers in Burkina Faso are rare and are often the result of Volunteers not taking preventive measures to stay healthy. The most common major health concerns in Burkina Faso are malaria, amebic dysentery, hepatitis, meningitis, and HIV/AIDS. Because malaria is endemic in Burkina Faso, Volunteers are required to take anti-malarial pills. You will also receive vaccinations against hepatitis A and B, meningitis A, C, W, and Y, typhoid, and rabies, if you are not already vaccinated against these diseases.

Other health problems in Burkina Faso are similar to those found in the United States, such as colds, diarrhea, headaches, dental problems, sinus infections, skin infections, minor injuries, STIs, emotional problems, and alcohol abuse. These problems may be more frequent or compounded by life in Burkina Faso because environmental factors raise the risk or exacerbate the severity of certain illnesses and injuries.

Helping You Stay Healthy

The Peace Corps will provide you with all the necessary inoculations, medications, and information to stay healthy. Upon your arrival in Burkina Faso, you will receive a medical handbook. At the end of training, you will receive a medical kit with supplies to take care of mild illnesses and first aid needs. The contents of the kit are listed later in this chapter.

During pre-service training, you will have access to basic medical supplies through the medical officer. However, you will be responsible for your own supply of prescription drugs and any other specific medical supplies you require, as the Peace Corps will not order these items during training. Please bring a three-month supply of any prescription drugs you use, since they may not be available here and it may take several months for shipments to arrive.

You will have physicals at midservice and at the end of your service. If you develop a serious medical problem during your service, the medical officer in Burkina Faso will consult with the Office of Medical Services in Washington, D.C. If it is determined that your condition cannot be treated in Burkina Faso, you may be sent out of the country for further evaluation and care.

Maintaining Your Health

As a Volunteer, you must accept considerable responsibility for your own health. Proper precautions will significantly reduce your risk of serious illness or injury. The adage "An ounce of prevention ..." becomes extremely important in areas where diagnostic and treatment facilities are not up to the standards of the United States. The most important of your responsibilities in Burkina Faso is to take the following preventive measures:

Falciparum malaria is endemic in Burkina Faso and the surrounding countries, so you are required to take malaria prophylaxis. The medical officers work with each Volunteer to provide the best prophylaxis possible. There will be more information on malaria and how to avoid it during pre-service training.

Many illnesses that afflict Volunteers worldwide are entirely preventable if proper food and water precautions are taken. These illnesses include food poisoning, parasitic infections, hepatitis A, dysentery, Guinea worms, tapeworms, and typhoid fever. Your medical officer will discuss specific standards for water and food preparation in Burkina Faso during pre-service training.

Abstinence is the only certain choice for preventing infection with HIV and other sexually transmitted diseases. You are taking risks if you choose to be sexually active. To lessen risk, use a condom every time you have sex. Whether your partner is a host country citizen, a fellow Volunteer, or anyone else, do not assume this person is free of HIV/AIDS or other STDs. You will receive more information from the medical officer about this important issue.

Volunteers are expected to adhere to an effective means of birth control to prevent an unplanned pregnancy. Your medical officer can help you decide on the most appropriate method to suit your individual needs. Contraceptive methods are available without charge from the medical officer.

It is critical to your health that you promptly report to the medical office or other designated facility for scheduled immunizations, and that you let the medical officer know immediately of significant illnesses and injuries.

Women's Health Information

Pregnancy is treated in the same manner as other Volunteer health conditions that require medical attention but also have programmatic ramifications. The Peace Corps is responsible for determining the medical risk and the availability of appropriate medical care if the Volunteer remains in-country. Given the circumstances under which Volunteers live and work in Peace Corps countries, it is rare that the Peace Corps' medical and programmatic standards for continued service during pregnancy can be met.

If feminine hygiene products are not available for you to purchase on the local market, the Peace Corps medical officer in Burkina Faso will provide them. If you require a specific product, please bring a three-month supply with you.

Your Peace Corps Medical Kit

The Peace Corps medical officer will provide you with a kit that contains basic items necessary to prevent and treat illnesses that may occur during service. Kit items can be periodically restocked at the medical office.

Medical Kit Contents

Ace bandages
Adhesive tape
American Red Cross First Aid & Safety Handbook
Antacid tablets (Tums)
Antibiotic ointment (Bacitracin/Neomycin/ Polymycin B)
Antiseptic antimicrobial skin cleaner (Hibiclens)
Band-Aids
Butterfly closures
Calamine lotion
Cepacol lozenges
Condoms

Dental floss
Diphenhydramine HCL 25 mg (Benadryl)
Insect repellent stick (Cutter's)
Iodine tablets (for water purification)
Lip balm (Chapstick)
Oral rehydration salts
Oral thermometer (Fahrenheit)
Pseudoephedrine HCL 30 mg (Sudafed)
Robitussin-DM lozenges (for cough)
Scissors
Sterile gauze pads
Tetrahydrozaline eyedrops (Visine)
Tinactin (antifungal cream)
Tweezers

Before You Leave: A Medical Checklist

If there has been any change in your health – physical, mental, or dental – since you submitted your examination reports to the Peace Corps, you must immediately notify the Office of Medical Services. Failure to disclose new illnesses, injuries, allergies, or pregnancy can endanger your health and may jeopardize your eligibility to serve.

If your dental exam was done more than a year ago, or if your physical exam is more than two years old, contact the Office of Medical Services to find out whether you need to update your records. If your dentist or Peace Corps dental consultant has recommended that you undergo dental treatment or repair, you must complete that work and make sure your dentist sends requested confirmation reports or X-rays to the Office of Medical Services.

If you wish to avoid having duplicate vaccinations, contact your physician's office to obtain a copy of your immunization record and bring it to your pre-departure orientation. If you have any immunizations prior to Peace Corps service, the Peace Corps cannot reimburse you for the cost. The Peace Corps will provide all the immunizations necessary for your overseas assignment, either at your pre-departure orientation or shortly after you arrive in Burkina Faso. You do not need to begin taking malaria medication prior to departure.

Bring a three-month supply of any prescription or over-the-counter medication you use on a regular basis, including birth control pills. Although the Peace Corps cannot reimburse you for this three-month supply, it will order refills during your service. While awaiting shipment – which can take several months – you will be dependent on your own medication supply. The Peace Corps will not pay for herbal or nonprescribed medications, such as St. John's wort, glucosamine, selenium, or antioxidant supplements.

You are encouraged to bring copies of medical prescriptions signed by your physician. This is not a requirement, but they might come in handy if you are questioned in transit about carrying a three-month supply of prescription drugs.

If you wear eyeglasses, bring two pairs with you – a pair and a spare. If a pair breaks, the Peace Corps will replace them, using the information your doctor in the United States provided on the eyeglasses form during your examination. The Peace Corps discourages you from using contact lenses during your service to reduce your risk of developing a serious infection or other eye disease. Most Peace Corps countries do not have appropriate water and sanitation to support eye care with the use of contact lenses. The Peace Corps will not supply or replace contact lenses or associated solutions unless an ophthalmologist has recommended their use for a specific medical condition and the Peace Corps' Office of Medical Services has given approval.

If you are eligible for Medicare, are over 50 years of age, or have a health condition that may restrict your future participation in health care plans, you may wish to consult an insurance specialist about unique coverage needs before your departure. The Peace Corps will provide all necessary health care from the time you leave for your pre-departure orientation until you complete your service. When you finish, you will be entitled to the post-service health care benefits described in the Peace Corps Volunteer Handbook. You may wish to consider keeping an existing health plan in effect during your service if you think age or pre-existing conditions might prevent you from re-enrolling in your current plan when you return home.

SAFETY AND SECURITY: OUR PARTNERSHIP

Serving as a Volunteer overseas entails certain safety and security risks. Living and traveling in an unfamiliar environment, a limited understanding of the local language and culture, and the perception of being a wealthy American are some of the factors that can put a Volunteer at risk. Property theft and burglaries are not uncommon. Incidents of physical and sexual assault do occur, although almost all Volunteers complete their two years of service without serious personal safety problems.

Beyond knowing that Peace Corps approaches safety and security as a partnership with you, it might be helpful to see how this partnership works. Peace Corps has policies, procedures, and training in place to promote your safety. We depend on you to follow those policies and to put into practice what you have learned. An example of how this works in practice – in this case to help manage the risk of burglary – is:

- Peace Corps assesses the security environment where you will live and work
- Peace Corps inspects the house where you will live according to established security criteria
- Peace Corps provides you with resources to take measures such as installing new locks
- Peace Corps ensures you are welcomed by host country authorities in your new community
- Peace Corps responds to security concerns that you raise
- You lock your doors and windows
- You adopt a lifestyle appropriate to the community where you live
- You get to know neighbors
- You decide if purchasing personal articles insurance is appropriate for you
- You don't change residences before being authorized by Peace Corps
- You communicate concerns that you have to Peace Corps staff

Factors that Contribute to Volunteer Risk

There are several factors that can heighten a Volunteer's risk, many of which are within the Volunteer's control. By far the most common crime that Volunteers experience is theft. Thefts often occur when Volunteers are away from their sites, in crowded locations (such as markets or on public transportation), and when leaving items unattended.

Before you depart for Burkina Faso there are several measures you can take to reduce your risk:

- Leave valuable objects in the U.S.

- Leave copies of important documents and account numbers with someone you trust in the U.S.

- Purchase a hidden money pouch or "dummy" wallet as a decoy

- Purchase personal articles insurance

After you arrive in Burkina Faso, you will receive more detailed information about common crimes, factors that contribute to Volunteer risk, and local strategies to reduce that risk. For example, Volunteers in Burkina Faso learn to:

- Choose safe routes and times for travel, and travel with someone trusted by the community whenever possible

- Make sure one's personal appearance is respectful of local customs

- Avoid high-crime areas

- Know the local language to get help in an emergency

- Make friends with local people who are respected in the community

- Limit alcohol consumption

As you can see from this list, you must be willing to work hard and adapt your lifestyle to minimize the potential for being a target for crime. As with anywhere in the world, crime does exist in Burkina Faso. You can reduce your risk by avoiding situations that place you at risk and by taking precautions. Crime at the village or town level is less frequent than in the large cities; people know each other and generally are less likely to steal from their neighbors. Tourist attractions in large towns are favorite worksites for pickpockets.

The following are other security concerns in Burkina Faso of which you should be aware:

Insert potential safety risks in the country

While whistles and exclamations may be fairly common on the street, this behavior can be reduced if you dress conservatively, abide by local cultural norms, and respond according to the training you will receive.

Staying Safe: Don't Be a Target for Crime

You must be prepared to take on a large degree of responsibility for your own safety. You can make yourself less of a target, ensure that your home is secure, and develop relationships in your community that will make you an unlikely victim of crime. While the factors that contribute to your risk in Burkina Faso may be different, in many ways you can do what you would do if you moved to a new city anywhere: Be cautious, check things out, ask questions, learn about your neighborhood, know where the more risky locations are, use common sense, and be aware. You can reduce your vulnerability to crime by integrating into your community, learning the local language, acting responsibly, and abiding by Peace Corps policies and procedures. Serving safely and effectively in Burkina Faso will require that you accept some restrictions on your current lifestyle.

Support from Staff

If a trainee or Volunteer is the victim of a safety incident, Peace Corps staff is prepared to provide support. All Peace Corps posts have procedures in place to respond to incidents of crime committed against Volunteers. The first priority for all posts in the aftermath of an incident is to ensure the Volunteer is safe and receiving medical treatment as needed. After assuring the safety of the Volunteer, Peace Corps staff response may include reassessing the Volunteer's worksite and housing arrangements and making any adjustments, as needed. In some cases, the nature of the incident may necessitate a site or housing transfer. Peace Corps staff will also assist Volunteers with preserving their rights to pursue legal sanctions against the perpetrators of the crime. It is very important that Volunteers report incidents as they occur, not only to protect their peer Volunteers, but also to preserve the future right to prosecute. Should Volunteers decide later in the process that they want to proceed with the prosecution of their assailant, this option may no longer exist if the evidence of the event has not been preserved at the time of the incident.

Crime Data for Burkina Faso

Crime data and statistics for Burkina Faso, which is updated yearly, are available at the following link: **http://www.peacecorps.gov/countrydata/burkinafaso**. Please take the time to review this important information.

Few Peace Corps Volunteers are victims of serious crimes and crimes that do occur overseas are investigated and prosecuted by local authorities through the local courts system. If you are the victim of a crime, you will decide if you wish to pursue prosecution. If you decide to prosecute, Peace Corps will be there to assist you. One of our tasks is to ensure you are fully informed of your options and understand how the local legal process works. Peace Corps will help you ensure your rights are protected to the fullest extent possible under the laws of the country.

If you are the victim of a serious crime, you will learn how to get to a safe location as quickly as possible and contact your Peace Corps office. It's important that you notify Peace Corps as soon as you can so Peace Corps can provide you with the help you need.

Volunteer Safety Support in Burkina Faso

The Peace Corps' approach to safety is a five-pronged plan to help you stay safe during your service and includes the following: information sharing, Volunteer training, site selection criteria, a detailed emergency action plan, and protocols for addressing safety and security incidents. Burkina Faso's in-country safety program is outlined below.

The Peace Corps/Burkina Faso office will keep you informed of any issues that may impact Volunteer safety through **information sharing**. Regular updates will be provided in Volunteer newsletters and in memorandums from the country director. In the event of a critical situation or emergency, you will be contacted through the emergency communication network. An important component of the capacity of Peace Corps to keep you informed is your buy-in to the partnership concept with the Peace Corps staff. It is expected that you will do your part in ensuring that Peace Corps staff members are kept apprised of your movements in-country so they are able to inform you.

Volunteer training will include sessions on specific safety and security issues in Burkina Faso. This training will prepare you to adopt a culturally appropriate lifestyle and exercise judgment that promotes safety and reduces risk in your home, at work, and while traveling. Safety training is offered throughout service and is integrated into the language, cross-cultural aspects, health, and other components of training. You will be expected to successfully complete all training competencies in a variety of areas, including safety and security, as a condition of service.

Certain **site selection criteria** are used to determine safe housing for Volunteers before their arrival. The Peace Corps staff works closely with host communities and counterpart agencies to help prepare them for a Volunteer's arrival and to establish expectations of their respective roles in supporting the Volunteer. Each site is inspected before the Volunteer's arrival to ensure placement in appropriate, safe, and secure housing and worksites. Site selection is based, in part, on any relevant site history; access to medical, banking, postal, and other essential services; availability of communications, transportation, and markets; different housing options and living arrangements; and other Volunteer support needs.

You will also learn about Peace Corps/Burkina Faso's **detailed emergency action plan**, which is implemented in the event of civil or political unrest or a natural disaster. When you arrive at your site, you will complete and submit a site locator form with your address, contact information, and a map to your house. If there is a security threat, you will gather with other Volunteers in Burkina Faso at predetermined locations until the situation is resolved or the Peace Corps decides to evacuate.

Finally, in order for the Peace Corps to be fully responsive to the needs of Volunteers, it is imperative that Volunteers immediately report any security incident to the Peace Corps office. The Peace Corps has established protocols for **addressing safety and security**

incidents in a timely and appropriate manner, and it collects and evaluates safety and security data to track trends and develop strategies to minimize risks to future Volunteers.

DIVERSITY AND
CROSS-CULTURAL ISSUES

In fulfilling its mandate to share the face of America with host countries, the Peace Corps is making special efforts to assure that all of America's richness is reflected in the Volunteer corps. More Americans of color are serving in today's Peace Corps than at any time in recent history. Differences in race, ethnic background, age, religion, and sexual orientation are expected and welcomed among our Volunteers. Part of the Peace Corps' mission is to help dispel any notion that Americans are all of one origin or race and to establish that each of us is as thoroughly American as the other despite our many differences.

Our diversity helps us accomplish that goal. In other ways, however, it poses challenges. In Burkina Faso, as in other Peace Corps host countries, Volunteers' behavior, lifestyle, background, and beliefs are judged in a cultural context very different from their own. Certain personal perspectives or characteristics commonly accepted in the United States may be quite uncommon, unacceptable, or even repressed in Burkina Faso.

Outside of Burkina Faso's capital, residents of rural communities have had relatively little direct exposure to other cultures, races, religions, and lifestyles. What people view as typical American behavior or norms may be a misconception, such as the belief that all Americans are rich and have blond hair and blue eyes. The people of Burkina Faso are justly known for their generous hospitality to foreigners; however, members of the community in which you will live may display a range of reactions to cultural differences that you present.

To ease the transition and adapt to life in Burkina Faso, you may need to make some temporary, yet fundamental compromises in how you present yourself as an American and as an individual. For example, female trainees and Volunteers may not be able to exercise the independence available to them in the United States; political discussions need to be handled with great care; and some of your personal beliefs may best remain undisclosed. You will need to develop techniques and personal strategies for coping with these and other limitations. The Peace Corps staff will lead diversity and sensitivity discussions during pre-service training and will be on call to provide support, but the challenge ultimately will be your own.

Overview of Diversity in Burkina Faso

The Peace Corps staff in Burkina Faso recognizes the adjustment issues that come with diversity and will endeavor to provide support and guidance. During pre-service training, several sessions will be held to discuss diversity and coping mechanisms. We look forward to having male and female Volunteers from a variety of races, ethnic groups, ages, religions, and sexual orientations, and hope that you will become part of a diverse group of Americans who take pride in supporting one another and demonstrating the richness of American culture.

What Might a Volunteer Face?

Possible Issues for Female Volunteers

Burkina Faso has a traditional, patriarchal society. Female Volunteers may be surprised by the extent to which community and domestic roles are defined along gender lines. Men generally hold positions of authority in the workplace (though women are becoming more visible there), in the community, and in the home. This can present challenges for female Volunteers, as the work they do may be seen as a typically "male" job. The difficulties are exacerbated because single women do not usually have the status and respect that comes with marriage and having children. Thus, women may find it challenging to have their ideas recognized and respected by both women and men.

Possible Issues for Volunteers of Color

Although Burkinabé society can be conservative, Volunteers generally find the Burkinabé to be hospitable and accepting of people with a wide variety of backgrounds. Nevertheless, Burkinabé may have preconceived notions of Americans based on the kind of information available in Burkina Faso about Westerners, which comes mainly from television, movies, magazines, and local news reports and often presents a limited view of American diversity. For example, Asian Americans are often called Chinois (Chinese), regardless of their actual background, and African Americans may not be considered Americans.

Possible Issues for Senior Volunteers

The high regard for seniors in Burkinabé society lends support to senior Volunteers' effectiveness at work. They, in turn, are able to find ways to use their extensive experience to assist their communities. However, seniors often comment that they feel a lack of camaraderie with other, mostly much younger, Volunteers. The three months of pre-service training can be particularly frustrating for seniors because of the rigid schedule, classroom setting, and issues of integration with other trainees in the group. Language learning may present an additional challenge. However, most senior Volunteers find living and working at their sites to be very rewarding.

Possible Issues for Married Couple Volunteers

The shared experience of serving as a married couple is incredibly rewarding. Many of the challenges single Volunteers face are different or non-existent for couples. However, there are potential difficulties that married Volunteers can face. Married Volunteers are advised to establish early a sense of individuality and do activities separately at their sites; otherwise, community members may not recognize their unique identities. When there are language proficiency differences between partners, it may be more difficult for the lower-level partner during the first few months of service. Married Volunteers who work to be independent in all work and social aspects of service are most successful and most content with their work. Because Burkina Faso cultural and historical norms, women face unique discrimination that men don't face. Among Volunteers, married couples are sometimes not accepted into Volunteer social circles, because their volunteer experiences are perceived to be different. Despite such problems, the shared memories are a gift that will unite couples for the rest of their lives.

Possible Issues for Gay, Lesbian, or Bisexual Volunteers

Given the society's conservative values, homosexuality is not likely to be tolerated by the general public in Burkina Faso. There may even be potential safety and security concerns. It is not possible to be open about your sexual orientation and maintain a positive working relationship with members of your community, and you will have to exercise extreme discretion. Other Volunteers and the Peace Corps staff will provide support, but you will find it very difficult to be open outside of that circle.

A recommended resource for support and advice prior to and during your service is the Lesbian, Gay, Bisexual & Transgender U.S. Peace Corps Alumni website at **www.lgbrpcv.org**.

Possible Religious Issues for Volunteers

Christianity, Islam, and indigenous belief systems all are represented in Burkina Faso. You will be free to practice your own religion as long as you demonstrate respect for the religion of the people in your community and refrain from proselytizing.

Possible Issues for Volunteers With Disabilities

As part of the medical clearance process, the Peace Corps Office of Medical Services determined that you were physically and emotionally capable, with or without reasonable accommodations, to perform a full tour of Volunteer service in Burkina Faso without unreasonable risk of harm to yourself or interruption of service. The Peace Corps/ Burkina Faso staff will work with disabled Volunteers to make reasonable accommodations for them in training, housing, jobsites, or other areas to enable them to serve safely and effectively.

As a disabled Volunteer in Burkina Faso, you may find that you face a special set of challenges. In Burkina Faso, as in other parts of the world, some people may hold prejudicial attitudes about individuals with disabilities and may discriminate against them. There is very little of the infrastructure to accommodate individuals with disabilities that has been developed in the United States.

FREQUENTLY ASKED QUESTIONS

This list has been compiled by Volunteers serving in Burkina Faso and is based on their experience. Use it as an informal guide in making your own list, bearing in mind that each experience is individual. There is no perfect list! You obviously cannot bring everything on the list, so consider those items that make the most sense to you personally and professionally. You can always have things sent to you later. As you decide what to bring, keep in mind that you have a 100-pound weight limit on baggage. And remember, you can get almost everything you need in Burkina Faso.

How much luggage am I allowed to bring to Burkina Faso?

Most airlines have baggage size and weight limits and assess charges for transport of baggage that exceeds those limits. The Peace Corps has its own size and weight limits and will not pay the cost of transport for baggage that exceeds these limits. The Peace Corps' allowance is two checked pieces of luggage with combined dimensions of both pieces not to exceed 107 inches (length + width + height) and a carry-on bag with dimensions of no more than 45 inches. Checked baggage should not exceed 100 pounds total with a maximum weight of 50 pounds for any one bag.

Peace Corps Volunteers are not allowed to take pets, weapons, explosives, radio transmitters (shortwave radios are permitted), automobiles, or motorcycles to their overseas assignments. Do not pack flammable materials or liquids such as lighter fluid, cleaning solvents, hair spray, or aerosol containers. This is an important safety precaution.

What is the electric current in Burkina Faso?

If you have electricity at your site, and it works, the current will be 220 volts, 50 cycles. Voltage sags and surges are very common and place a real strain on power supplies and voltage transformers or regulators. The Peace Corps does not provide transformers or regulators to Volunteers. Many Volunteers use rechargeable batteries with a solar charger, which is a good alternative to disposable batteries.

How much money should I bring?

Volunteers are expected to live at the same level as the people in their community. You will be given a settling-in allowance and a monthly living allowance, which should cover your expenses. Volunteers often wish to bring additional money for vacation travel to other countries. Credit cards and traveler's checks are preferable to cash. If you choose to bring extra money, bring the amount that will suit your own travel plans and needs.

When can I take vacation and have people visit me?

Each Volunteer accrues two vacation days per month of service (excluding training). Leave may not be taken during training, the first three months of service, or the last three months of service, except in conjunction with an authorized emergency leave. Family and friends are welcome to visit you after pre-service training and the first three months of service as long as their stay does not interfere with your work. Extended stays at your site are not encouraged and may require permission from your country director. The Peace Corps is not able to provide your visitors with visa, medical, or travel assistance.

Will my belongings be covered by insurance?

The Peace Corps does not provide insurance coverage for personal effects; Volunteers are ultimately responsible for the safekeeping of their personal belongings. However, you can purchase personal property insurance before you leave. If you wish, you may contact your own insurance company; additionally, insurance application forms will be provided, and we encourage you to consider them carefully. Volunteers should not ship or take valuable items overseas. Jewelry, watches, radios, cameras, and expensive appliances are subject to loss, theft, and breakage, and in many places, satisfactory maintenance and repair services are not available.

Do I need an international driver's license?

Volunteers in Burkina Faso do not need an international driver's license because they are prohibited from operating privately owned motorized vehicles. Most urban travel is by bus or taxi. Rural travel ranges from buses and minibuses to trucks, bicycles, and lots of walking. On very rare occasions, a Volunteer may be asked to drive a sponsor's vehicle, but this can occur only with prior written permission from the country director. Should this occur, the Volunteer may obtain a local driver's license. A U.S. driver's license will facilitate the process, so bring it with you just in case.

What should I bring as gifts for Burkina Faso friends and my host family?

This is not a requirement. A token of friendship is sufficient. Some gift suggestions include knickknacks for the house; pictures, books, or calendars of American scenes; souvenirs from your area; hard candies that will not melt or spoil; or photos to give away.

Where will my site assignment be when I finish training and how isolated will I be?

Peace Corps trainees are not assigned to individual sites until after they have completed pre-service training. This gives Peace Corps staff the opportunity to assess each trainee's technical and language skills prior to assigning sites, in addition to finalizing site selections with their ministry counterparts. If feasible, you may have the opportunity to provide input on your site preferences, including geographical location, distance from other Volunteers, and living conditions. However, keep in mind that many factors influence the site selection process and that the Peace Corps cannot guarantee placement where you would ideally like to be. Most Volunteers live in small towns or in rural villages and are usually within one hour from another Volunteer. Some sites require a 10- to 12-hour drive from the capital.

How can my family contact me in an emergency?

The Peace Corps' Office of Special Services (OSS) provides assistance in handling emergencies affecting trainees and Volunteers or their families. Before leaving the United States, instruct your family to notify the Office of Special Services immediately if an emergency arises, such as a serious illness or death of a family member. During normal business hours, the number for the Office of Special Services is 855.855.1961, then select option 2; or directly at 202-692-1470. After normal business hours and on weekends and holidays, the OSS duty officer can be reached at the above number. For non-emergency questions, your family can get information from your country desk staff at the Peace Corps by calling 855.855.1961.

Can I call home from Burkina Faso?

International phone service to and from Burkina Faso is quite good. The national telephone company, ONATEL, has offices in all of Burkina Faso's administrative towns. Calls to the United States are expensive, so most Volunteers arrange to receive calls from home or limit calls to providing call-back information, so the receiver can return the call. Many Volunteers also send text messages to friends and family to arrange calls. U.S. calling cards cannot be used in Burkina Faso, and calling collect is not possible.

Should I bring a cellular phone with me?

Basic cell phones can be purchased inexpensively in Burkina Faso. Most American cell phones do not work in Burkina Faso. Cell phone service is expanding rapidly and most Volunteer sites are now covered.

Will there be email and Internet access?

Computer access is available at private Internet cafes in many towns and cities and, for work-related purposes, at the Peace Corps office. Wireless coverage, when available, can be slow. Unlocked smart phones that use SIM cards can provide Internet access almost anywhere.

Should I bring my computer?

The decision whether to bring a laptop computer depends on your own needs. Among the factors to consider are that computers are not required for Volunteers' work; the Peace Corps does not provide technical support or insurance for personal computers; you may not be assigned to a site with electricity; and, as mentioned above, computer access is available at Internet cafes and at the Peace Corps office. However, most Volunteers who have brought laptops with them have been happy with their decision and have used their computers for both personal and work-related purposes. Volunteers recommend bringing an external hard drive or big flash drive and computers with long battery life. In smaller villages, there may not be electricity, but there are almost always places to charge electronics for a small fee.

WELCOME LETTERS FROM COUNTRY VOLUNTEERS

Congratulations!

You're on your way to becoming a Peace Corps Volunteer in Burkina Faso and beginning what likely will be the greatest adventure in your life so far. You've probably been waiting with anticipation for months, maybe even years, for this adventure to begin, and I know you've come a long way to get here. Well, I can tell you that if you open yourself up to the process, dedicate yourself to the experience, and keep an open mind and positive spirit, you will not be disappointed!

Everyone's experience here is different: Some live in a city while many live in small villages; some speak only in French while others speak more local language; some work regular weekday hours and others work more sporadically. But regardless, everyone's experience is what they make of it. Remember that old saying: What you give is what you get. It doesn't get truer than here in the Peace Corps. If you are committed to pushing yourself out of your comfort zone, trying new things, and bridging new cultural barriers, you'll make some of the most unique friendships of your life and, as they say in one of my favorite songs from Wicked, you will be changed for good.

At this point in the process, you're probably feeling a mix of emotions: anxiety, excitement, nervousness, stress, and maybe even sadness at the thought of leaving everyone you love and the comforts of home. Well, this mix of emotions, and many more, will probably ebb and flow and change and resurface throughout your service as you move from one day to the next, and then one year to the next. But through it all, remember that Peace Corps is a two-year process for a reason. Be patient with yourself. You will make mistakes, and that's OK, because in the end you will learn French. You will learn your local language. You will become a leader in your community. And, in time, you'll learn to love your new home in Burkina Faso.

So enjoy your last few weeks at home, live in the moment, and don't forget to laugh and have fun!

Bridget Roby, Health Volunteer

Dear New Volunteer,

Congratulations on being invited to Burkina Faso! You're probably very excited, nervous, and stressed right now. Don't be. The people here (other Volunteers, Peace Corps staff, and locals) are all very welcoming and helpful. Don't worry too much about what to pack; you can buy most things you will need in-country. Don't stress about things like language either. You will be just fine; the PC staff is very helpful and professional.

The Peace Corps is all about learning. When you are here, you learn from everyone around you, and everyone around you learns from you. No matter what your background is you have something to offer. The most important lesson you will learn here is that everything will work out. Communication can be difficult but you will become fluent in the universal language of hand gestures and body language. You will learn very quickly to just let things go and go with the flow. These are the most important lessons you will learn in the Peace Corps and you will have a great time learning them.

The work can be fun and rewarding and very challenging. You will get out of your experience what you put into it. So if you are willing to work hard and have fun with people, you will have a very rewarding experience no matter your background in French or traveling or working.

The Peace Corps is a very unique experience with lots of ups and downs. You will have great days and horrible days. But the good days always outnumber the bad ones, and there are always other Volunteers, staff, and friends in your village who want to help you and are always willing to listen.

We aren't changing the world, but we are changing lives and, in the process, changing our own lives. So welcome to the family!

Barb Franco, Health Volunteer

Ne y waongo!

Welcome to Burkina Faso, the land of the upright people! As a volunteer, you will be able to experience this firsthand as well as aid in the development of the country itself. You will soon find that there is always something to do whether it be sector activities or cultural exchange and, in the long run, they are both equally fulfilling.

While Burkina Faso is one of the poorest countries in the world, the majority of people are amazing, and they continually demonstrate this trait; whether it's by inviting you over for dinner (usually rice, beans, pasta, or a local dish called tô, made by boiling flour [base of millet, corn, yams, or plantains], and then garnished with one of several sauces), chatting on the street, or by serving as a host family and welcoming you into their house.

There are most definitely challenges here; among them are heat, the language barrier, and different amenities than what we are used to in the United States. But, winter isn't going anywhere (and it's nice to get a break from it sometimes). One of the national languages here is French and chances are that you will be learning one of many local languages as well; learning at least one new language is a skill you will be able to keep with you for the rest of your life. And, there are new amenities that you can enjoy such as appreciating the company of people for hours on end and seeing some of the clearest stars that you will ever see. Also, you will be helping people to expand their horizons, develop their capacities, and make their country a better place. In short, you will be making a difference: While you might not always be able to see it, it's always important to remember.

Most importantly, the volunteers here are a big family. We all support each other, we want each other to succeed, and we are all extremely happy that you are coming to join us.

You might be nervous, stressed, or apprehensive about coming—and you're completely justified: Joining the Peace Corps is a big deal. Just enjoy your last few weeks at home, keep a positive attitude, and expect the unexpected.

Welcome to the family, we look forward to seeing you soon!

Andrew Smith-Freedman, Health Volunteer

Thank You.

By coming to Burkina Faso, you will be helping people I care about, people who have become my dearest friends, who have embraced me as family and who I have embraced in return, who I have laughed and cried with, seen born and seen die. Even if I never meet you—even if our times in Burkina Faso do not overlap—I want to thank you for the decision you have made and for the decision you will remake every day until you return home after your service.

You're probably looking for some advice, and a small part of you somewhere is wondering why I haven't congratulated you. The two are related, so let's get straight to the advice:

Peace Corps service is not about you. It's not about me, either. You have not yet met the people whose lives you will change, and you may not even realize it when you do so, but your service, like mine, is about them. Mother Theresa said, "If you can't help a thousand people, help just one," and your service will be a success from the moment you touch a life in any way, even by saying hello. Don't worry about it. Success is guaranteed. It's just not about you.

An RPCV (that's returned Peace Corps Volunteer—both the Peace Corps and the Burkinabé love acronyms so get used to it) of my acquaintance was asked by his mother what the hardest part of his service had been. Was it pooping in a hole or flies or mosquitoes or illness or daily exposure to poverty? Was it long bike rides or missing

American food or slow Internet? What about the fear of being robbed or being the only white person in town? "No," he said, "it was the culture."

She then asked him what the best part of his service was. Smiling, he said, "The culture." I can't tell you which of the physical realities here in Burkina will be particularly challenging to you, but I can tell you that people will do things that will completely astound you, frankly have you tearing your hair out with confusion and frustration and when you ask why, they'll say, "C'est comme ça ici."("It's like that here.")

Another key phrase is "Ca va aller," meaning "It will go" or, more to the point, "Things will work out." People here live for today, for this moment, for now. Sometimes that's wonderful. Sometimes it means the stores don't have change, the bus is three hours late, and the village hasn't fixed the water pump before dry season. Welcome to culture.

So, how can you prepare for all this craziness? How to get ready for a seismic shift in your environment? The ancient Greek sages, as usual, have good advice: "Know thyself." In Burkina, you will be more yourself than anywhere else. Things that have always been true become not different, but more true. Your weaknesses will be unmasked and your strengths more wonderful than you can imagine.

The Peace Corps is not about you, but only by knowing your own strengths and weaknesses can you make the most of it for these wonderful people you have yet to meet and care about. And no matter what you find, know that there is a Peace Corps family here waiting to welcome you, a culture waiting to fascinate you, and a country waiting for you to fall in love with it.

You have an incredible community waiting for you. Welcome home!

Elijah LaChance, DABA Volunteer

PACKING LIST

This list has been compiled by Volunteers serving in Burkina Faso and is based on their experience. Use it as an informal guide in making your own list, bearing in mind that each experience is individual. There is no perfect list! You obviously cannot bring everything on the list, so consider those items that make the most sense to you personally and professionally. You can always have things sent to you later. As you decide what to bring, keep in mind that you have an 100-pound weight limit on baggage. And remember, you can get almost everything you need in Burkina Faso.

General Clothing

- Professional clothes to wear in public, at the Peace Corps office, or to meetings (nice pants, blouses, nice button-down shirts, not a suit and tie, but business casual wear is good—Burkinabe have much respect for those who dress well)

- Clothes you want to wear to go out at night

- Note on skirts—they have to cover your knees when you sit, but they don't have to be floor length. Many people wear skirts and dresses but it's not necessary if you really don't like them

- Comfortable clothes to wear in village (T-shirts, comfortable skirts, pants—you don't need to dress like you're going hiking/camping. Sleeveless shirts are fine just avoid things that are tight, low cut, or ratty)

- Linen clothes are very nice, but you can also get linen clothes here

- One or two pairs of jeans (no holes, nothing ratty)

- One or two pairs of comfortable lightweight pants or long capris (one pair of workout capris would be good for biking. You also might want lightweight pants and a top for sleeping.)

- One to two pairs of shorts for around the house

- Good quality underwear and bras (not the underwear in a bag)

- Two or three pairs of socks if you like to go running

- Comfortable sweater (cold season is cold when the sun goes down)

- Scarves (nice ones can be found here as well)

- Baseball cap or wide-brimmed hat

- Breathable, lightweight rain jacket

- Swimsuit (there are swimming pools in the capital and other cities)

- Belt (you may lose weight and need one to hold up your pants)

- Your favorite jewelry, but nothing too dear to you

Shoes

- Comfortable sandals: one "fancy pair" and flip flops (Chacos or Tevas if you already wear them in the States)

- Lightweight running shoes, if you're a runner

Very important: Don't bring anything that you can't bear to see destroyed by the dusty climate, harsh soap, and merciless hand-washing.

Personal Hygiene and Toiletry Items

- Bring a three-month supply to get you through training

- Deodorants (very hard to find your favorite here)

- Soap holder

- Shampoo and hair conditioner (two-in-one shampoo comes in handy with limited water)

- Face wash

- Lotion

- Toothpaste (Colgate is available all over the country)

- Razor and a supply of razor blades (available here, but expensive)

- Foot care items (Sorry, but your feet will get trashed, so you may want a pumice stone and other exfoliating devices; you can find inexpensive shea butter and shea butter products here)

- Face sunscreen

- Waterproof Band-Aids

- Diva cups (menstrual cups) are great here

- Cosmetics and hair accessories (mascara, bandanas, etc., if you use them)

- Nail polish

Miscellaneous

- Sturdy backpacks. Day packs (some like fanny packs or the tops of larger packs) are nice for work and bike rides. Medium packs are good for short trips. Large packs are recommended for longer trips (if you plan any) and getting all your stuff here.

- A good quality head lamp (Petzel)

- Solar lamp (for reading and general lighting: "Firefly" made in Uganda)

- Batteries for your battery-powered items, rechargeable batteries and a solar recharger or one that works with local current (Solio brand charger works very well). Batteries here are of poor quality.

- IPod and speakers (solar powered by Goal Zero)

- A couple pairs of headphones

- Leatherman or Swiss Army knife

- Bug hut

- Bag/solar shower

- Good can opener (cheap ones can be found here)

- Zip-top bags (in various sizes)

- Good pens and craft supplies (special papers, permanent markers, highlighters, pencils, pastels, etc.)

- Good non-stick frying pan and plastic spatula (can be found here, but are expensive)

- Sharp kitchen knife (if you plan on cooking, this is essential; knives here are very dull; you may even want to bring a knife sharpener)

- Family pictures and anything from home that will make you feel more comfortable—again, don't bring items too dear to you

- Eyeglass repair kit

- A watch, if you use one (Volunteers often use cell phones bought here for clocks and alarms)

- Vegetable peeler

- Musical instrument (if you play or would like to take up a new hobby)

- Travel-size board games (Scrabble, Boggle, etc.)

- Playing cards can be nice for playing with children in your village or other Volunteers

- Small towel or a special pack light towel (a piece of cloth bought in Burkina serves just as well)

- If you're at all picky about pillows, bring your own

- If you plan on biking extensively, you may want to bring biking accessories, such as a padded seat

- Teachers, bring your calculators

Burkina Faso is a very dusty country, so it is a good investment to purchase protective covering for any electronic devices you bring.

Books

Do not worry too much about books. There are plenty of books already here. Kindles and other e-readers are very popular with Volunteers.

Food

- Powdered drink mixes (e.g., Starbucks Via, Crystal Light, or Kool-Aid; sugar is available here)
- Powdered sauce/flavor/condiment packets
- Your favorite spices
- Your favorite snack and junk foods
- Sugarless gum, if you're a chewer

You can conserve packing space by preparing a package with food, books, and anything else you may not require right away during training and sending it to yourself c/o the Peace Corps office.

Things not to bring

- IPad (no USB drive)
- Medical supplies (i.e., ibuprofen—all essentials provided by Peace Corps)
- Shoes that you wouldn't wear in the U.S. (Chacos, Keens, Tevas are not for everyone. If you like them, bring them; if you don't like them normally you won't wear them here.)
- Cheap sunglasses (can be found everywhere here; bring nice ones if you want them)
- Dishes, utensils, etc.
- French dictionary (provided by the Peace Corps during training)

PRE-DEPARTURE CHECKLIST

The following list consists of suggestions for you to consider as you prepare to live outside the United States for two years. Not all items will be relevant to everyone, and the list does not include everything you should make arrangements for.

Family

- Notify family that they can call the Peace Corps' Counseling and Outreach Unit at any time if there is a critical illness or death of a family member (24-hour telephone number: 1-855-855-1961, then press 2; or directly at 202-692-1470).

- Give the Peace Corps' On the Home Front handbook to family and friends.

Passport/Travel

- Forward to the Peace Corps travel office all paperwork for the Peace Corps passport and visas.

- Verify that your luggage meets the size and weight limits for international travel.

- Obtain a personal passport if you plan to travel after your service ends. (Your Peace Corps passport will expire three months after you finish your service, so if you plan to travel longer, you will need a regular passport.)

Medical/Health

- Complete any needed dental and medical work.

- If you wear glasses, bring two pairs.

- Arrange to bring a three-month supply of all medications (including birth control pills) you are currently taking.

Insurance

- Make arrangements to maintain life insurance coverage.

- Arrange to maintain supplemental health coverage while you are away. (Even though the Peace Corps is responsible for your health care during Peace Corps service overseas, it is advisable for people who have pre-existing conditions to arrange for the continuation of their supplemental health coverage. If there is a lapse in coverage, it is often difficult and expensive to be reinstated.)

- Arrange to continue Medicare coverage if applicable.

Personal Papers

- Bring a copy of your certificate of marriage or divorce.

Voting

- Register to vote in the state of your home of record. (Many state universities consider voting and payment of state taxes as evidence of residence in that state.)
- Obtain a voter registration card and take it with you overseas.
- Arrange to have an absentee ballot forwarded to you overseas.

Personal Effects

- Purchase personal property insurance to extend from the time you leave your home for service overseas until the time you complete your service and return to the United States.

Financial Management

- Keep a bank account in your name in the U.S.
- Obtain student loan deferment forms from the lender or loan service.
- Execute a Power of Attorney for the management of your property and business.
- Arrange for deductions from your readjustment allowance to pay alimony, child support, and other debts through the Office of Volunteer Financial Operations at 855.855.1961, extension 1770.
- Place all important papers—mortgages, deeds, stocks, and bonds—in a safe deposit box or with an attorney or other caretaker.

CONTACTING PEACE CORPS HEADQUARTERS

This list of numbers will help connect you with the appropriate office at Peace Corps headquarters to answer various questions. You can use the toll-free number and extension or dial directly using the local numbers provided. Be sure to leave the toll-free number and extensions with your family so they can contact you in the event of an emergency.

Peace Corps Headquarters Toll-free Number: 855.855.1961, Press 1 or ext. # (see below)

Peace Corps' Mailing Address: Peace Corps Headquarters
1111 20th Street, NW
Washington, DC 20526

Questions About:	Staff:	Toll-Free Ext:	Direct/Local #:
Responding to an Invitation	Office of Placement	x1840	202.692.1840
Country Information	Melaney Monreal-Starling Desk Officer / (Burkina Faso, Mali, Niger & Uganda) burkinafaso@peacecorps.gov	X2612	202.692.2612
Plane Tickets, Passports, Visas, or other travel matters:	CWT SATO Travel	x1170	202.692.1170
Legal Clearance	Office of Placement	x1840	202.692.1840
Medical Clearance & Forms Processing (includes dental)	Screening Nurse	x1500	202.692.1500
Medical Reimbursements (handled by a subcontractor)	Seven Corners	N/A	202.692.1538 800.335.0611
Loan Deferments, Taxes, Financial Operations	Office Of Volunteer and PSC Financial Services	x1770	202.692.1770
Readjustment Allowance Withdrawals, Power of Attorney, Staging (Pre-Departure Orientation), and Reporting Instructions	Office of Staging *Note: You will receive comprehensive information (hotel and flight arrangements) three to five weeks prior to departure. This information is not available sooner.*	x1865	202.692.1865
Family Emergencies (to get information to a Volunteer overseas) 24 hours	Office of Special Services	x1470	202.692.1470